THE CARDS I WAS DEALT

Stacie Carr

ISBN 978-1-63903-495-6 (paperback)
ISBN 978-1-63903-496-3 (digital)

Christian Faith Publishing, Inc.
832 Park Avenue
Meadville, PA 16335
www.christianfaithpublishing.com

Printed in the United States of America

ACKNOWLEDGMENTS

First and foremost, this book is all for my Lord and Savior Jesus Christ. Without him, I wouldn't be able to tell my story. Without his grace and mercy, this book would not be possible.

> With God all things are possible. (Matthew 19:26)

> But the LORD has become my stronghold, and my God the rock of my refuge. (Psalm 94:22)

To Lauren, my nurse, who taught me compassion and patience. Thank you for being my lifelong friend.

To my three angels: Tina, Barbara, and Julie, who were mothers when mine was not there. Thank you for taking care of me like true moms when I needed caring for the most.

To Mr. Tobias, for never letting me slack off and always being my cheerleader. You guided my way through high school with full confidence I would succeed and reach my goals.

Last but certainly not least, my parents. Thank you for always being there for me especially in times where I needed it the most. You've taught me how to be a great person and a great mom. Thank you for walking me through life holding my hand and guiding my faith.

PREFACE

My story starts on April 26, 1985.

Up to the point of 1997, my life was great. It was full and happy. My family was close. My family consisted of my parents and my siblings, a brother six years younger, and a sister two years younger.

I grew up in a small town where most of my family lived. We lived in a house my daddy built in 1986 on the outskirts of town. We had room to run and had a pool. I changed schools a few times in elementary school but ended up at the school my grandma worked for.

We started a new church in April of 1997, and it quickly became family.

Through all of the story, you're about to read my faith is what held me up. I knew that God had me in his arms, and his angels were always by my side.

> I can do all things through Christ who strengthens me.
>
> —Philippians 4:13

CHAPTER 1

1997

It was June of 1997, and I was promoted to seventh grade. I would miss the normalcy of the same teacher and the same people around campus. I would miss my friends I had become accustomed to seeing day in and day out. I was very social, but the thought of new people and changing classes every hour freaked me out. I guess it is the only time in my life where I was shy.

Starting a new church life after attending the same church for my life up until this point is a little nerve-racking. After attending a wedding, we felt like this was our new home. We quickly got comfortable and adapted to our new family.

My parents found it important that at the ages we were, we get plugged into a good church. Lucky for us, the church we visited for a wedding would be our new family. We were all very involved in the church, from cleanings and being representatives on the boards, and even being the day-care provider. Looking back, I appreciate that I have this extended family I am still close with to this day.

Summer was finally here, and my new church encouraged beach camp for the upcoming junior high kids. Getting involved in the youth was what everyone did. Camping at the beach for a week with my new family, I was excited to get to know everyone on a more personal level.

August came quickly and it was time to head out without my parents for an entire week with people I really didn't know. Looking back, it was kind of weird to know my parents allowed me to go off with people we all barely knew. Since it was with a church group, maybe it was comforting for my parents.

We had devotions a couple times a day. It was a church camp after all. We played games every night and contests. We rode skateboards and flew big kites that had two handles. I got a try at the kite; I was lifted off the ground before Bubba came and pulled me down.

I don't remember a lot of the trip. Just pieces.

I remember waking up in the trailer one morning, and my eyes were watery. I tried to rub it, out and when that didn't work, I tried to blink it out. Behind my eyes was a pain I've only had once before that I can remember. The first time, I was in third grade, and a friend rubbed my temples with little relief. I probably ended up going home. In the morning, I woke up with the blinding, literally, headache.

We had our surprise trip. We were going to Catalina. I've never been to Catalina, and I didn't know how we were going to get there or what we would do when we got there. I was excited for the new adventure. Tina, my mom on this trip, helped me get ready and helped me eat.

We drove up to Long Beach and got on a ferry. My headache was worse at this point, and I didn't think it could've gotten worse than it already was. I get motion sickness, so Tina gave me some Advil and Dramamine as a precaution for the ferry ride. I got sick anyways.

Once we got to the docks, I was much worse. The group took a picture, and the small group of moms and dads that I was part of went to get something to eat at a Mexican food restaurant. We didn't get too far on the island before I was put into a lounge chair in a courtyard. The courtyard was surrounded by small trinket shops and a pharmacy. Tina and two more moms, Barbara and Julie, started to feed me pain medication. Tylenol, Advil, aspirin, or Motrin didn't touch the headache.

There were talks of taking me home when we got back to the mainland if I didn't improve. This group of parents are my angels. I still to this day talk to them and praise them for being my comforters.

When we got back to the mainland, we got some KFC. Everyone sat on the freshly cut green grass overlooking the Pacific Ocean. The breeze was slight but smelled of salt and water. The breeze hit my face and made the headache rage. I did eat a little but quickly threw it all up. It was a decision I was not part of, but the adults made it. Julie would take me home since she was heading that way.

It was pitch-black, but my parents stood at the front porch with all the houselights on. Daddy came and picked me up out of the car and took me to my room. The next steps probably didn't happen the way I remember, but this is my story from my perspective. I was taken to urgent care at some point after I got home. The doctor told my mom I was of age to start my period, and it was most likely a migraine.

The days dragged on, and I wasn't getting any better. By this point, I was not eating, barely walking, and couldn't see. It was obvious to my parents that it had something to do with my eyes. They took me to see an eye doctor at Walmart in Poway. I don't remember the details or even going through the eye check. My eyes burned so badly I could barely make it through the appointment. My parents' dogs started following me everywhere. I couldn't go anywhere with the two of them right next to me. They would follow me all day and sleep in my bed and on my pillows with me.

Next was seeing my primary doctor. She already knew what was going on because of the eye doctor. I do not know how much time passed before my primary doctor sent me for an MRI. Again I really did not remember the entire process. I do remember the doctor stabbing me with an incredibly large needle. Maybe he was having a bad day since it was early on the weekend, and we pulled him away. He jabbed that incredibly large needle in my butt.

In my daddy's arms, I was a pile of mush walking into a very bright-white lobby. People walked around with their hands in their faces. People sat at the edges of the room on small benches.

After eleven hours of surgery, the ICU needed to prepare my parents for what I would look like. He sat down with them at the worst possible time and explained that eleven hours of open brain surgery would take a toll on my fragile little twelve-year-old body. He told them I would have tubes and wires all over. I would be attached to several machines, but it was all normal. By God's pure grace, I had no wires or no tubes. I had one IV and the oxygen tubes in my nose and one machine.

Fast-forwarding to when I woke up. I couldn't see, but it didn't stop the nurses from shining light on my face, poking and prodding and throwing nonstop questions that filled my throbbing head. Why couldn't I see who was touching me and bothering me with that stupid light?

What was going on? Where was I? Why was I here? Why couldn't I see?

During the eleven hours of surgery, I suffered a stroke. My neurosurgeon took my dad and went over the scans. Dr. Barba, my neurosurgeon, showed my dad the infarcts the strokes had caused. The infarcts had made spots in my brain that showed I had had a stroke during the surgery.

I'm not sure when I learned what happened or what was going on. I was moved to a new area with lots of other beds. The room was wall-to-wall beds. Beeping from machines, sobs from others in the room, and other kids in hospital beds. My bed was against a wall, facing the wall-to-floor windows out looking Hillcrest. I was not used to the city, but the big buildings were a sight for this country girl's eyes.

I had this wrap around my head and a tube sticking out of my head. The pain was more tolerable, and I could finally see. Every time I moved, the nurse had to come and adjust the tube in my head. The needle in my hand was more painful than the head pain. I couldn't lie on my hand to sleep. Needless to say, I was uncomfortable.

Every few hours, no matter the time, I was woken up and asked the same questions: "What's your name?" "Do you know where you are?" "Do you know why you're here?" "What day is it?" The light never went away. The nurses were constantly shining a bright light in my eyes. It was like looking into the sun for those three minutes.

At some point, the tube in my head came out, and I could get out of the room. Daddy put me in a wheelchair and pushed me around outside where we found the best coffee stand. It was kind of our morning thing, just him and me. I did go to the cafeteria a few times. I don't care what anyone says about hospital food; I really enjoyed it. Maybe I enjoyed getting out of the room. Maybe it was the social side of me being able to see people.

Most of the time, people who came to visit brought food. Daddy and Mom went and got food for the most part, enough for the nurses too. We found the best pizza place that was a couple blocks from the hospital; I think that was my favorite.

Friends and family showed up with stuffed animals, flowers, balloons, gifts, and food. I had tables set up in my little corner. We were separated only by sheets, so I am sure I was encroaching on someone else's space. My best friend and I were obsessed with Winnie the Pooh, and mostly everything that was brought was some shape or form of Pooh things. I still have a couple things from back then in my house. My daughter has my big plush Pooh and Eeyore.

The nonstop traffic of people that came to visit was indescribable: friends, family, teachers, principals, and my new church family. There were so many gifts and so much food my small area was cramped. People would come and stay with me to give my parents a break. I remember my sixth grade teacher, Mr. Croman, and my elementary school principal, Mr. Tiegs, came and sat with me so my parents could take a break. "It is like a revolving door of visitors," my nurse Lauren told my parents. She wasn't kidding. Between family, friends, neighbors, and church family, there was always someone there. Mountains of stuffed animals and the food; the food was like a twenty-four-hour buffet.

The rounds of medications and scan seemed to never end. On one of the CT scans, the machine was having problems, but they proceeded with it anyway. They told my nurse she couldn't go in with the clip in her hair because of the magnet in the machine. She didn't care and came in anyway. It caused problems with the machine, so unfortunately, she had to leave. The usual fifteen-minute scan took a long time. I think it lasted a total of forty-five minutes. During those forty-five minutes, I had my first near-death experience.

I was in my hospital bed being pushed down an awkward hallway. My grandmother I have never met held my hand through the halls. The hallway reminded me of the hallway in *Beetlejuice*. It wound one way and directly the next. The hallway was narrow but didn't have straight lines. It was sort of dark but with a fluorescent lighting like in an interrogation room. People sat on the benches against the walls, and the doors weren't uniform. A door opened, and it was red and dark, and the heat rushed out and touched my face. My grandmother pushed the foot of my bed away and said, "Not this one." I continued down the hallway staring at my feet at the end of the hospital bed. I remember the white hospital blanket that covered me. The next door opened to a blue-and-white room. It looked like I opened the door of an airplane. The blue was the sky, and the white was perfectly formed clouds, like the ones the Care Bears were on.

A man walked out from the clouds, not a stranger but a man I knew. The olive skin and perfect face with long brown hair stretching past his shoulders. All I could think was, *This is it. I know it. You only see him when it is your time.* My Maker, my Creator, my God. His hand reached out for mine, but he just stood there looking at me. Was he waiting for me to reach out? He said, "It's not your time." The door closed softly, almost a whisper. I woke up.

Was that a premonition? Was it a dream? Nonetheless, I was greeted by my parents and my nurse Lauren. The hallways of the hospital were different from my dream. These hallways were bright and white. No people sat on a bench in the hallways, and the doors were all open.

My night nurse woke me up for the routine annoying questions and the damn light in my face. When Chris woke us up that early morning, our TV was on, and he told us Princess Diana had died. It was crushing to my mom, who adored her. It was bad enough we were there to find out the news but that someone so beautiful inside and out had been killed in a car accident. Chris was my nighttime Lauren.

To this day, I compare all my hospital visits to the eighth-floor IMU. I barely opened my mouth to speak when a nurse was right at my side. They were like genies; anything I wanted, I got. My nurse, who was my personal genie, was always there. We became very close and still hold a relationship over twenty years later. I was her personal dress-up doll. She painted my nails and toes and did my hair as best as she could.

When my neurosurgeon, Dr. Barba, came in, he would ask the same questions the nurses bothered me with. Dr. Barba told me that since my hair was so long and beautiful, he didn't want to shave it off, so they just shaved a small strip from ear to ear. He came in with a flock of white coats one time and thought he would be funny by asking me an abnormal question, maybe just to see how alert I was. He asked, "What is the capital of Nevada?"

I just finished elementary school. Of course, I knew the answer. "Carson City." *Of course*, I was thinking. *Duh, that was an easy one.* Yet the flock stood there with inquisitive looks on their faces. They all said different answers from Las Vegas to Reno. Lauren had to burst their bubbles and ensure the twelve-year-old was correct. They were mind-blown that none of them knew the correct answer. When it came time to change my head wrap, my neurosurgeon asked how I wanted my hair "Up, half-way up or all down?"

Days went by with the same routine. My favorite was my morning walk and coffee with Daddy. After eleven long days, I was finally released for the cushion of a full-time staff. People whom I didn't even know were praying for me. People my parents worked with who weren't religious were praying for me too. To me, this was God's way of bringing those people closer to him. I like to think that, because of the situation going on, God used me to bring people close.

CHAPTER 2

MAKE-A-WISH

The following summer, a friend of ours had told us about the Make-A-Wish Foundation and what they are all about. On the Make-A-Wish website, the foundation says, "For children diagnosed with critical illnesses, a wish come true can be a crucial turning point in their lives. A wish can be that spark that helps these children believe that anything is possible and gives them the strength to fight harder against their illnesses. This impact is why we are driven to make every one of these wishes come true." I fit the criteria. Although, I was not as severe as others, and others deserved it more than I did.

At first, my mom wasn't sure that it was such a good idea. Unlike our friends, I didn't have a life-threatening disease like their children. After basically being talked into accepting the fact that I was indeed one of those children, we were soon referred to by this family.

Later, we had gotten a call from Jim, a Make-A-Wish colleague, saying he wanted to meet with us and talk about the chance of getting me a wish. The first time I met with him, I had no idea what it was all about. I was left out of the loop as far as accepting the chance to make the decision. When Jim had come to the house, I had no idea why he was there or who he was. Jim just seemed to me like a guy asking a lot of questions. When Jim asked me, "If you could have any wish in the entire world, what would it be?"

I had my Miss America moment and said, "If I could make one wish, what would it be? For the world to be a more peaceful place to live." Jim just laughed and told me what he was there for. He explained that it was more of a material thing he could give me.

Although meeting someone famous was mentioned, he highly recommended I didn't go that route.

I finally decided after thinking about it that I wanted to do something with my family. I chose to go on the Big Red Boat Cruise and to Walt Disney World.

We stayed at Disney World for three days and stayed in the Dixie Landing, a very nice hotel on the Disney grounds, and the theme was the Splash Mountain characters. We were given Make-A-Wish T-shirts and buttons to wear at the parks.

The first day, we went to the Epcot Center, where they had all different origins from around the world, places like Germany, Sweden, Japan, China, Italy, and more. They had a few rides; after all, that was why we were there. The countries didn't fascinate us as much as the rides. We waited in line for Test Track, and a cast member saw us and asked if we were with the foundation on a wish trip. Of course, we told her yes, and she told us that we were special guests and didn't need to stand in line on our visit. She directed us in the back door where we went to the front of the line. It was like we were celebrities. Cast members treated us as such. At nighttime, there was a light show in the middle of all the countries in the pond. The water changed colors; it splashed up into fountains of brilliant changing colors. The fireworks show is the best I've ever seen.

The second day, we went to Magic Kingdom, which is just like Disneyland in California. The Magic Kingdom was missing some of our favorite rides but offered different rides in lieu of them. This day, my knee was bothering me from a previous stunt. I don't remember what I did, but the doctor told me I pulled something in my knee. It was swollen and tender, and I couldn't walk for long periods of time. We rented a wheelchair, which made my mom even more uncomfortable. She thought it made my illness look worse, and people would think I was bound to the wheelchair, and that's why I was there. Wearing our Make-A-Wish shirts and buttons again, we were again treated like royalty throughout the park.

Last day, we went to MGM Studios, much like Universal Studios. There weren't many rides there but tours and shows. There was a *Honey, I Shrunk the Kids* Land. We felt like we were actually in the movie. Grass standing taller than anyone, bugs the size of bears, and sprinklers the size of the Empire State building. We went to the stage show of Doug, the cartoon from the nineties. We got to meet and take pictures with the entire cast.

After those couple days at Disney World, we went on the cruise. Back then, it was the Big Red Boat. We, of course, wore our Make-A-Wish attire and again were treated like royalty. The characters were not Disney characters because the ship was not in partnership with Disney. Disney had recently acquired their own ship but was unknown to us when I made my wish. The cast on the ship was Looney Tunes. Much like Disney, the characters walked around in costume. I don't remember the ship or what we did.

The cruise took us to the Bahamas. We docked at Nassau and looked around, and it is a normal place, except their water is blue and clear as crystal. Downtown was beautiful with brightly colored buildings and amazing people. The people were kind and lively. My sister and I got our hair wrapped by a beautiful Bahamian woman with a stand in the downtown square.

We slept in the boat and enjoyed our night playing games, meeting people, and hanging out in the pool. There was assigned seating in the dining room, and we sat with a couple and their grandson. We enjoyed the time with the three of them and spent our time with the grandson around the ship.

The next day, we went to Pleasure Island with many of the people from the boat. At Pleasure Island, my family and I got the chance to swim with the dolphins. We got to ride on their backs, swim with them, play with them, and they pushed us up out of the water while we rode on their noses. I remember the cast constantly had to fish tiny little jellyfish out of the water with large nets. The lagoon where the dolphins were was separated from the ocean only by a thick net. The rest of the day we spent relaxing and enjoying the barbecue. A couple of my family members went snorkeling.

I was sorry to leave the most beautiful place I have ever been to, but all good things must come to an end.

CHAPTER 3

JUNIOR HIGH

When we got home, I had some catching up to do. All of my friends had started seventh grade. Once I was cleared by the doctor, I could go back. I was anxious about starting even more than before.

I just now realized after a thought of thought that I had changed. I changed into a new girl that was shy and needed the approval of those whom I wanted to befriend. I needed to be liked by all no matter the cost. My surgeries made me insecure of who I was now. The thought of people looking at me and seeing me differently haunted my every thought. I had become insecure.

The first day back, I was the *new girl*. Even though some people knew me, I was the girl who came in late. Everyone knew about my condition—perks of being in a small town, I guess. I was wearing headbands to cover my scar. It was not really the *in* thing, but it was the only way besides a hat to cover my scar.

Trying to handle the seven classes was overwhelming. I was trying to fit in with my old friends who already had their groups. I felt like a minnow in a sea of sharks. I was always being looked at sideways and pointed at like I was something special. I guess they didn't know how to handle someone who had a medical issue. My friends were very welcoming and invited me into their groups that I was now a part of.

The first day was overwhelming. I ended up going home early and staying home for another few weeks. I guess I just needed the comfort of home and my mom. I don't remember doing work at home to keep up, but when I did eventually go back, I was failing all my classes. That was a punch to the gut since I have never failed at anything. It took a while to catch up and be comfortable in my new surroundings. I eventually fell into step and found my rhythm. I was still the "sick" girl for a long time, and people treated me as such. People were helping guide me around, watching my steps for me, holding my trays, and guiding me from class to class.

Teachers all knew about my situation, so they were always helpful and overly nice not to offend me or make me uncomfortable. The school nurse, where I spent a lot of time, was also helpful with making my situation more comfortable. She introduced me around the office and told me about another girl who was in the same situation. If I ever needed to talk, I knew where to go.

School dances were part of the experience. I went to every dance I could possibly go to. It was extra time with my friends, and let's not forget we got to dance one of my all-time favorite things.

Seventh grade went by quickly to the point I don't remember much. Once eighth grade came around, I had my footing, and many more of my friends joined the junior high world. I was the upper-grade girl now. I had boyfriends on and off. We went to dances together, had lunch together, and would go out on the weekends. We would write notes in between classes. I was getting the groove about being an independent girl.

I was succeeding in everything at thirteen. I was active in after-school dances and friends on the weekends. My grades were good, my teachers liked me, and I was social. Okay, so I wasn't doing great in all my classes, but I was passing and doing my best. I was still seeing my neurosurgeon and getting scanned every few months. I was given a clean bill of health every time. The doctors were just keeping an eye on everything. I was off all my medications and having no problems.

Eighth grade went by in a blur, and high school was quickly approaching. The anxiety was back. Starting all over. I was comfortable about my place in the junior high world.

CHAPTER 4

2001

This was a long year, medically and personally. I had my first boy-friend, and we went to my first high school dance as a couple. Being hopeful that nothing medically would happen again, I enjoyed high school and the social part of it as much as anyone. The relation-ship didn't last long past Christmas, but after a tearful couple of days, I moved on.

Got another boyfriend later the next year and another surgery in my future. The doctors tried several different medications to keep my headaches at bay, but in the end, all they did was make me look like a blowfish and made my hair fall out. I don't remember actually going into the hospital or the events leading up to it.

My hospital stay was a few days shorter than my first stay. Yet all the same, I was royalty there. I got a new nurse, Mei-Mei, whom I quickly became friends with. She was there when Lauren wasn't. Some of the nurses would walk up to the foot of the hospital bed and talk to me like we've met. They would remind me that they met me the last time I was there, but I don't remember. I don't know if it was the open brain surgery or the fact that people had been digging in my brain, but some of the memories are just lost. When my Lauren wasn't there to be my genie, I had other great nurses playing the role.

Although Lauren was always my first choice since we had a bond, she was there for all of my brain tumor surgeries. Besides my parents, she was my rock and biggest cheerleader—still holding the award for best nurse ever in my book. She still tended to my medical needs as well as my pampering needs.

I didn't get my same cozy corner like I did the first surgery, but this time, I got a window space. Still that little country girl, the view never ceased to amaze me. The buildings stood tall, casting shadows on the street below. The cars still rushed by, and traffic backed up every morning and every night like clockwork. The lights of the city at night were my favorite.

I still got my favorite pizza from the Bronx down the street. The best pizza in San Diego in my opinion. The nurses still ate great with my parents around too. They wouldn't allow me to leave until I pooped. My nurse Mei Mei said if I didn't do it on my own, she'd have to do something about it. I guess going to the bathroom is important. They measured every time I went to the bathroom. Medicine came in forms of pills and IVs. They thought the medicine was making my stomach problems worse. I must have eventually gone since I did go home.

The recovery was different this time. I wasn't in my childhood home and all the comforts of it. Family came over and babysat when my parents or boyfriend weren't there. I needed to be watched carefully for a few weeks after my surgeries to make sure I didn't have a seizure or didn't fall.

Started my sophomore year of high school. I went to another big dance with some friends—and boom, the tumor struck again. I can remember lots of ER visits and lots of morphine. Again the medicines to keep my headaches away didn't work. More doctor appointments and another surgery.

Third surgery was coming up and, hopefully, my last. This was by far the worst one physically. Same routine in the hospital.

After I got home, my physical appearance was horrifying. My face was all puffy from the steroids. My stomach was swollen from the steroids like I was pregnant, even hard. My eye was shut, leaving me with one eye. Not my good eye either.

I can remember it being close to Halloween time, and my mom and I went to the market for groceries, and I looked like a heinous monster. People stared, people pointed, but no one ever came up and asked what happened. I can only guess the assumptions. My face was puffy and bruised, my eye was swollen shut, and I wore a yellow Hurley baseball cap.

One couple did actually ask what happened. Without a skip, I replied, "I got in a fight." My mom stared in awe and shook her head. *She was mortified*, I thought to say something like that.

"Stacie Elizabeth!"

Okay, I was caught. But before I could tell them the truth, the guy said, "I'd hate to see the other person." I couldn't help but giggle at the thought of me—of all people—getting into a fight where the result was me looking like a monster from a horror story.

Confession time, I guess. I told the couple what really happened, and they were more shocked at the truth than the lie. The "Oh my gosh," "You're so lucky," "Wow" were flooding out of them like a leaky faucet. I don't know what is worse, the shock of the truth or the pity on their faces. The man said, "Well, at least you've already got a Halloween costume. You could be Mike Tyson. All you need is a fake ear attached to your mouth." I am glad I put off the aura of not being offended by remarks such as that. I went along with it and laughed. It really didn't hurt my feelings. I am glad other people could find humor in the situation as I did.

My cousin used to sit in front of me for hours telling me to open my eye. With all my strength, I tried to open it to please him. He would then pull my eyelid up and tell me to keep it up.

My eye eventually opened a little, and no one was more excited than my little cousin. He would tell everyone who would listen, "Stacie's eye is open." After a while, it eventually opened all the way, but my eyeball was stuck in the corner. It made my already bad eyesight worse. From my first surgery, I was blind from the middle of both eyes to the left; at least that's when I noticed it.

The tumor was on my left optic nerve and was strangling it. I lost my vision from the middle of both eyes to the left. I was having to go through physical therapy because the strokes left my left side lame. From the huge needle that was shoved in my butt, I struggled with a sciatic nerve that was hit in that process. I used to get up at all hours of the night to sit in my parents' jet tub with the jet pulsating my sciatic nerve areas, as far as side effects that wraps it up. These are all things that I still struggle with today. The left side of my body does its own thing. My hand will creep up and lie on my breast, or when it is holding something, it tightens into a fist. My left leg twitches and kicks by itself. You can imagine how hard it is for me to get my nails done with my hand constantly turning and tightening.

My eye stayed stuck in the corner for a long time, it seemed. I went on a date, and we went to the movies. I noticed my eye focused when I was concentrating on something. It made me kind of dizzy, and I grabbed my sister who was with me and ran up the long staircase to the bathroom. I looked at my reflection in the mirror and focused like I did on the movie, and there it was: my eye had pulled itself back into place.

I was being homeschooled once again by the same old tall man who would come collect my schoolwork and return it to the school. I actually did do my work. The only teacher who actually came to my house was my Spanish teacher because she said I actually needed to be taught. It didn't look like I was going to go back to school anytime soon even though it was only October.

I got a call from the high school telling me I was failing all my classes except Spanish. How is that even possible if I have done my work and given it to the teacher they assigned for me? The only conclusion I could come up with was that he wasn't turning in my work! I think that was the turning point, and I had to go back to school, but not the high school because now I had almost a year and a half to make up for, and the counselor at the high school told me there was no way I would catch up.

I started school at the academy in town, which allowed me to go to school a couple times a week and part-time at home. I did my work and showed up to class to turn in my homework. I worked with the teacher when needed; it's not like they actually stood in front of the class to teach. It was all independent work, which was great so I could do my work, and the teacher was there to help. I didn't work well on my own, so staying at that school didn't last but a few months.

On to the next school. I needed to be in a classroom with a full-time teacher to keep me going. On to Montecito High School, which was an alternative high school. You know one of those high schools the "bad kids" go to? I was nervous like any other time starting a new school. The stares and wonder from the other students made me self-conscious. First day, I had a teacher sit down with me and look at my transcripts and go over in detail where I stood. I was at the end of my sophomore year with freshman credits because my work had not been turned in. He said, "You are behind, but if you work really hard and show up to class every day and attend my night classes for extra seat time, you can graduate on time." That was my first sight of hope. To this day, Mr. Tobias still holds a special place in my heart. He never gave up on me and continued to push me the next two years.

All the teachers at my new school were all so encouraging and helped me meet my goals each quarter. I spent all my time doing schoolwork and working. Working gave me extra credits toward graduation. Both the schools I was at before Montecito had no faith I could amount to anything, especially graduating on time.

My first job was at Burger King with my best friend. It worked out well since I only lived down the street and could walk to work. I only took orders at the cash registers, so I was only in one place and not moving around the kitchen causing problems with my vision. I loved working there. It was always busy, and I loved the interaction with the customers and coworkers.

CHAPTER 5

2002

The doctors think they got it all. At least there were no more brain surgeries in my future. The last surgery did a number on my face. Aside from my eye shutting and being stuck in the corner, I had some drooping and muscle deformities. From the middle of my forehead to the high of my temple, the muscle that stretches there was now in a puddle under my temple. My face was significantly drooping on the right side as well. Being that *insecure girl*, I needed it fixed immediately.

So much for no more surgeries.

We found a plastic/reconstructive doctor who would do the work: partial face lift, shaving of some muscle, and an implant in my temple. Sounded easy to me. I mean, I've had brain surgery; this should be a walk in the park. The face lift was to lift the droopy part on the right side. The temple reconstruction was to add an implant to help cover the ginormous indent on my right temple. They thought by shaving the muscle and adding the implant, it wouldn't be so noticeable. But it was and still is noticeable to me.

It was such a traumatic experience for my family and me that the specifics are a little bit all over the place. We can't remember when exactly the surgeries took place. It was the first quarter of the year is all I can be certain about.

I was comfortable with the plastic surgeon since he was at the campus of the hospital. I all but considered my home away from home. I know it's sad that the hospital would be considered so, but I not only felt completely at home at UCSD but loved being there.

After my surgery, like all my others, my head was fully wrapped in gauze. It was a bit more painful than my brain surgeries. It hurt to touch my face; forget about when it itched. It felt like I was numb and could never really get the satisfaction. Unlike the brain surgeries, I wasn't on the eighth-floor IMU. I was in my own room off the same floor. My old nurses would pop in when they were working to come chat and catch up. It was a different experience not being able to call a nurse by their name and have them magically appear at the foot of the bed.

I had a call button. I don't remember much other than those small details of the surgery or being in the hospital. I do remember he sent me home with this face/head-wrap thing. I had to wear it at night to help push my muscle down into its new home under my temple. The first night I slept with it on, it ended up around my feet. It didn't last long wearing the silly contraption; it would never be on in the morning.

I was excused from school by all my teachers, who all kept in touch and checked up on me frequently. They all had complete faith I would catch up, which I did. My boyfriend at the time brought me my books and kept everyone in the loop as far as my recovery. I still didn't feel right and okay with my looks, but my surgeon said he wouldn't touch me again because of the risks of the muscle falling more. I cried because I didn't feel he did what I thought of as a complete job; it still looked bad.

We found another surgeon who would do it, but I wouldn't go to UCSD for recovery. That was unnerving. This new surgeon would do the outpatient surgery at a children's hospital. He also worked with operation smile in third world countries to help children with facial deformities. We liked him much better. He was more compassionate and personal than my previous surgeon.

Here we go again. He basically did the same surgery less than a year later: pulled my face back, put in an implant, and shaved more muscle off. This time, it was an in-and-out surgery, so I didn't have to stay at the hospital for any length of time. Recovery was a few weeks, then it was back to school to do all the catching up I needed to do. Seat time matters.

I went to prom with my boyfriend and some friends; we got a limo! I was excited I got to get dressed up and dance all night long. There were things we could do with the high school like major dances, and I didn't want to miss any of it. I missed my friends who were there, but I got to experience the important things of high school.

CHAPTER 6

2003

I got my license! I turned eighteen, and after some begging and meetings with the safety guy at the DMV, I was a licensed driver. My surgeon wasn't happy he had to give his okay, and he didn't think it was the safest idea, but it was my rite of passage. My first car was a 2001 green Ford Mustang.

Last leg of school. Not only was I almost caught up, but I was making straight As, which sucked for my dad because he made a deal that for every A, we got $50. Still the other schools that had no faith that I could not only catch up but be doing it with good grades—joke's on them. I not only was working and kicking major ass at school, but I graduated on time with honors. No, I didn't become valedictorian, but I took almost every scholarship.

I worked at the school district and I was the student representative for my school, I had a certain pull with the superintendent. I would go monthly to the school board and tell them the happenings at my school through a PowerPoint presentation I made. They were impressed every month with my knowledge and tenacity to do such a thorough job (their words).

When time came for graduation, I was disappointed my GPA had not gotten up far enough for me to be valedictorian. I had so much to say and praise to give to my teachers at Montecito. A few phone calls and a little pull got me a speech spot. I received an award from the school board for my time served as a student representative. With the award, it landed me a thank-you-speech spot. It was more than that to me.

After school, I went to work at the Boys and Girls Club as a staff member. I loved kids, and it was the perfect job for me. I didn't work full-time. They opened a new wing of the club at the middle school for the teens after school. I was moved there and was much happier with the kids there. I was in charge of the girls' dance time. Since I had taken a dance class instead of a PE class from seventh to tenth grade, they thought the spot fit me well.

I was on my way to my boyfriend's house to go shopping with his mom and got in my first accident. I was in my mom's brand-new Toyota Highlander. I turned on the road from a light, and an elderly woman turned into me. I didn't see her since she was on my left side, but it ended up being her at fault. From that moment, my mom insisted I get a bigger car that sat up off the street more than my Mustang.

We went truck shopping. I didn't want anything too big because I was afraid it was going to obstruct my view or be too hard to maneuver. I wanted an Explorer Sport, but that wasn't big enough for my mom. We found a stepside crew-cab black Ford F-150. It was on the bigger side, but I felt comfortable and higher up in it. It didn't take long to feel comfortable or enjoy the feeling of being high up and big. Plus, it had room for my goddaughter.

CHAPTER 7

2005

My sister's cheer team was good. Like so good we were in Florida at least once a year for several years in a row. When I made my wish, my parents told me that I should pick something they would never be able to give me. Going to Walt Disney World and a cruise was that. Fast-forwarding several years, my sister would not only be a cheerleader but a damn good one.

We found ourselves at Walt Disney World again and again for years to come. Her team was good. We spent four days at the resorts with thousands of cheerleaders. We went to competitions for a few hours then spent the rest of the time at the parks with my sister and her friends.

We were heading home on Valentine's Day and got to the airport back home sometime during the evening. I had to go back to work the next day—yay. We all went home as a family and got home semi-late.

Not exactly sure what happened the next day since what I am about to tell you will play a part in it. The following day was the sixteenth of February, and I had a doctor's appointment because I was having a hard time sleeping and feeling rested when I did get to sleep. I only remember that and the next several days because someone filled in the spaces. On my way to the doctor's office, I fell asleep driving at seventy miles per hour. Remember from the previous chapter, I was now driving a midsize truck. I hit some gravel and overcorrected, assuming I was kind of awake at this point. I was driving the wrong way on the wrong side of the road and slid into a tree. Someone must've stumbled across the accident or heard it happen and then called 911.

Crews came to rescue me from my all-so-mangled truck. They had to cut the tree I hit down to cut the top and side of my truck off in order to get me out. The impact from the tree smashed me into my center console. I was cut out of my favorite jacket and on a stretcher and transferred by helicopter to the nearest trauma hospital. My daddy still has those pieces of my jacket.

My mom got a call from my sister, who got a call from her boyfriend, who got the call from his best friend, who happened to be the tow-truck driver. Did you follow that? I grew up in this same town, so it was a small community, and everyone heard everything. My mom called my boyfriend's mom, and they decided to each take a hospital since no one knew where I was. It happened so fast that the police hadn't even contacted my parents yet. I was told that people from my church were there when I woke up, including my pastor. The secretary at the church wanted to make sure I had a familiar face to wake up to.

I had a broken pelvis in three places, including my tailbone, and had a severe concussion, so the next several days and weeks are filled in by people and a little by memory. My truck was unrecognizable. I had a close family friend tell me that he saw my truck and didn't know it was mine. He said he told his son that whoever was in that truck didn't make it. Come to find out it was me and that I did, in fact, live, he said my angels were working overtime.

I was walked around with a walker through the hospital halls. It was complete torture. It was the worst pain I have ever experienced in my life, including my brain surgeries. I couldn't sit, I couldn't stand, and I most definitely couldn't walk even with the walker that helped stabilize me.

I had to get a hospital potty chair, a hospital shower chair, and a donut. I was being babysat and watched like when I had my brain surgeries. I couldn't do anything but lie to be comfortable. My boyfriend's mom took care of me the most since I lived there. She showered me and drove me around. I couldn't have driven if I had to. I could barely walk, let alone drive at this point.

I eventually went to a cane and got rid of the walker and wheelchair. I was still having a problem standing without something, and sitting was the worst. To add to the pain of sitting anywhere, especially in my truck, I lived on a bumpy dirt road.

We went to a family funeral in May, and I was still using a cane. The terrain was so rough at the family cemetery I could barely walk with a cane. I gave up after a while and started walking with little to no help. That was the day I kicked the stabilizer.

Somewhere in my healing process, Daddy took me truck shopping. It needed to be bigger than the last one because all my parents were firm, and it had to be a Ford since that is what protected me from getting hurt. I give full thanks to God for being the one who saved me. This time, I couldn't be the one to test-drive since I was still broken. Daddy was more than happy to do it for me. We left with my new fire-engine red, supercrew, full four-door 2005 Ford F-150. It was beautiful.

For my twentieth birthday, I got it lifted! To this day, it is the most beautiful truck to me, even though I don't have it.

In another story, the in-between will be told. This year was a big life-changer, a turning point for me.

CHAPTER 8

2006

I broke up with my boyfriend of four years in July. The year started out not great, but little did I know by the end I would meet my soul mate. My orthopedic warned me not to get pregnant for a few years in order to allow my pelvis to heal correctly. Well, God had other plans. I was pregnant by the end of the year despite taking numerous precautions. A lot happened in a few short months, and it is in detail in the following book. I had gotten married and had a baby by the end of summer 2006. Like I said, a lot happened in the few short months following my near-fatal car accident. Without going into too much detail, 2006 was a huge year and nothing medically happening.

We were on our way to my aunt's to make my wedding invitations at the end of March. I just found out I was three months pregnant and had gotten engaged the week before. We were on Highway 15 going north toward Murrieta, and a car drove perpendicular across the freeway from the Pechanga Exit. People were slowing down, so Daddy, who was driving, started to slow down. The car came to a halt in the middle of the fast lane, and we were trapped and couldn't move fast enough, and we hit the car. The car was pushed almost to the center median. I don't think anyone had hit us from behind. My fiancé was thrown forward since he was lying down, and the seats caught him. I don't remember the rescue squad coming, but they must have, and once the accident was to the point where we could leave, we did. We drove to the nearest hospital to get checked out. The hospital was packed, and we sat in a hallway on chairs waiting for our turn. After what seemed like forever, we decided to leave to go to another hospital.

We headed back toward home to a hospital we were more familiar with. We told the hospital I was pregnant, and they hurried us back. My fiancé went to another room to get checked out and I in another to get examined. By this point, his family was there. The doctor came in and gave me a quick check and was about to send me home when someone told him to check on the baby. He said there was no one there who could do a sonogram, but he could use the heartbeat doppler. The doppler rolled from one side of my belly to the other with nothing. From top to bottom, he checked with no heartbeat. Our hearts dropped. My sister-in-law had to walk away in order to not show me the tears. After about fifteen minutes and a change of body position, there it was, a heartbeat.

I got married and had a baby by October. I had to have a C-section since there was no way of knowing the stability of my pelvis. I stopped working and became a full-time mom and wife, still living with my parents. I was driving home after getting my brother and his friend from school. A car was stopped at the stop sign to my right, and at the last possible minute, it pulled out in front of me. I grabbed the wheel and turned as far as I could without hitting another car, but the car pulled out in front of me. CRASH!

I had my brother, his friend, and my new baby in the car. I later found out my brother didn't have his seat belt on but jumped on top of the baby in case glass shattered. The officer said the other people were talking and probably just broke a hip, but they were both okay.

I threw my hand up that day and said, "God, I get it. I will stop driving." After now three car accidents, not including the one where my daddy was driving, and with my vision problems, I gave up driving that day. December 20, 2006, was the last time I drove a car.

I heard from the officer who responded to the accident. He had paperwork to fill out, and he was checking on us. He informed me that the driver was a ninety-four-year-old lady and that she had passed. He assured me that I didn't kill her and that the accident was not my fault. This started my anxiety and depression journey.

CHAPTER 9

NEW ADVENTURE

Things were looking up. We found our own place, and it was perfect for us. It was an apartment attached to my grandparents' workshop. I was also going to be celebrating a one-year birthday party for my baby.

The next day, we had a family member losing his house in the landslides, and he needed help getting what he could. My husband had brought an Italian-imported wood table with six chairs in our new home.

We celebrated my baby's first birthday in October even though it was a month late, but we needed to have our own place to celebrate. We had family and friends over for the birthday party at our new place. We had been working around the yard the weeks before, and we wanted to have it finished before we had the party.

The next day, we went to my cousin's rodeo in the Country Estates, and the wind was really blowing. On our way home, we noticed a fire behind the hill of our new house. We watched it for a bit before my husband said we needed to grab a few things and leave, just in case. We grabbed a few pairs of clothes and some of the birthday presents and some favorite toys. Remember, we lived with my parents up until this point, and everything we had in the new place was brand-new and still in boxes. We had things from my husband's childhood that were given to us at the baby shower. We grabbed what would fit in the truck and left, not knowing what would be left when we came back.

We went to my parents' house to keep ourselves safe. We watched the fire from across the valley. The fire crawled down the hills and into the valleys. The winds were still roaring, and now it was feeding the fire. Soon after arriving at my parents', we got the call we had to leave. Lucky for us, we lived right near the road to take us off the mountain. Off to another safe place we went.

My mother-in-law lived in the city, and we knew it would be a safe place. The entire night was filled with yells and tears. My hometown was on fire, and we probably lost our house. But we were safe and together. It was about 4:00 a.m. when my mother-in-law came to wake us up and told us we had to leave—there was another fire.

We loaded up what things we did have and headed for another safe place. We went to my aunt's in Menifee this time. We had taken the motorhome since my parents and siblings were also told to leave. We made camp at her house with her and her husband and their five kids. We were safe and out of harm's way from the fires, but we were surrounded. It was like we were in a valley surrounded by fire and smoke. From every direction you looked, there was smoke billowing up into the sky and hills around us. We had even considered going to Arizona to my aunts. Southern California was engulfed in flames, and we really weren't safe. We stayed for about two weeks until it was clear enough to go home, or what we hoped would be our home that we left.

We couldn't get up to our new home just yet, so we went to my parents' house. Their house was still standing, but the fires burned to the edge of our property. We heard that the firefighters felt our home was the safest since there was more than ten feet of clearance from the brush. They took refuge and fought the fire from our house. The French doors had been blown open, and there was ash in a blanket across the living room and kitchen.

When we were finally able to go to our new place, my husband and his best friend went up there knowing there was nothing left. My grandpa and uncles stayed and fought the fire and protected the main house, but by the time they looked back at the workshop, it was engulfed in flames. I couldn't bring myself to go up and see it. It was not only my first home with my family, but it was my childhood filled with memories of it. They took pictures and grabbed what things were left. To this day, we have a tub of things that were found: things like plates and silverware and a colander.

We carry it around as a reminder of where we started and what we have grown to by the grace of God. People from our church pulled together and gave us necessities. We bounced from house to house for a while. We weren't taking things around with us since we lost everything. It was a hard transition for a while, but our love and faith got us through. Let's not forget the many people and family members who had our backs.

CHAPTER 10

2009

This was another tough year for me personally. Nothing medically—thank you, Jesus! No accidents either (remember, I stopped driving).

By this year, I had been married almost three years and had a baby who was almost three. We still lived with my parents on the hill with my brother and sister too. It was a big house, and we all had our own space.

My grandpa had been sick and in and out of the hospital for a few months. He had gone into the hospital and later passed away. This was a hard one for me because I was close with my grandpa. My heart was broken that I had lost him, but I was happy he wasn't struggling any longer.

March and April came, and by this time, my sister moved out and moved to Maryland with my aunt and uncle. She missed my birthday, and so did my parents. They all made up for it early the next morning. They called at 6:00 a.m. California time and yelled "HAPPY BIRTHDAY" in the phone. My sister and I had become close while she was away. We talked on the phone every day and never forgot to say "I love you."

My husband and I celebrated our three-year anniversary; and about ten days later, I lost my sister—my best friend, the godmother to my son. My sister had been struggling with drug addiction for some time by this point. She went to Maryland to rehab herself until she felt she could do it on her own. That's when she came back to San Diego.

She came back and fell into her old habits and her old friends. She had found a place that would have room for her in a week, so we think she decided to live it up until then. Kind of like going on a diet and splurging before you start.

We got a phone call early in the morning. I remember thinking it was too early for someone to be calling. I heard voices on the answering machine. I rolled over and went back to sleep. There was a knock at the door a while after, and it was Daddy saying we needed to talk as a family. He grabbed my brother from his room and took us to his bedroom and shut the door.

My mom looked like she was sick, and she was lying under the covers. Daddy had a sick look on his face too; he spoke quietly like he was trying to keep whatever it was a secret. He said, "It's bad! It's your sister. Your sister died this morning."

Maybe I was in shock, but just then, my mom broke out in tears uncontrollably. I hugged her as tight as I could wrap my arms around her.

My brother just did what my brother does when faced with a tragedy. He shrugged and said something like he wasn't surprised. We left the room, and I had to go find my husband. He was outside in the garage. I opened the door with, I am sure, a complete, sick look on my face. He grabbed me and asked what was wrong, and I just burst into tears and collapsed to the ground, hitting my knees. "She's gone. She's gone. My sister is dead." He just took me in his arms and held me until I could stop shaking.

I had to be the strong one now and make some plans and phone calls. I knew my parents wouldn't be up to it, so I had to swallow my pain and step up. I made phone calls and sent messages.

Soon after we heard the news ourselves, my pastor was informed. He stopped whatever it was he was doing with other church members and raced up to our house. He grabbed my dad and hugged him and sobbed alongside my dad. No words were right, so they just hugged and sobbed some more.

My heart was empty. My head was flooded, but things needed to get done. I made plans. When time came for her services, the church was packed, standing room only and overflowed outside.

Every room in the church was full. Her friends, my friends, church family, and family stood together, embracing and comforting one another. Pastor could not control his emotions and got choked up, and the tears started to fall. It was hard for all of us. Soon after saying goodbye to my sister, I found out I was pregnant again.

We were all suffering from the deaths that surrounded us, but we couldn't stay holed up. People had to work and fulfill their duties. The next couple of months were a fog. Learning to live without two people I loved and them not being there anymore was hard. October came around, and my papa was sick and in and out of the hospital. Papa was sick, and he passed away. Our wounds were still open from the last two deaths, and we had to add another. We had services for Papa and said our final goodbyes.

Soon after, my parents were losing their house. The house I brought my baby home to. It was the beginning of 2010, and I had my second child, and we were packing up my parents' house. At this point, we were living on our own in Escondido, my family of now four. My little family couldn't stop getting sick. Both kids had been seen at children's hospital in San Diego and diagnosed with a respiratory problem. We did a little investigation and found we were having a mold problem in our apartment and needed to move ASAP.

Since my parents had lost their house, they were living at my grandma's, and that's the only place we had left to go. My parents' trailer was there, so my family of four moved into the trailer. We celebrated my new baby's first birthday in the snow. Soon after, my husband had back surgery and was laid up. By this time, my parents had their own place, and we lived in the house. We were all getting used to our new way of life, and my husband was recovering from surgery when my grandma got notice she was losing her house. We had found ourselves practically homeless again. My grandma bought a new house, so we went with her temporarily. My husband was still recovering from surgery, and we were down to just whatever he was making on disability. We couldn't get a place of our own on what he was making.

We ended up getting money from the accidents and fire and were able to get our own place. He wanted to be closer to work, so we settled on a place in Escondido again. This time, it was a townhouse with a tiny yard that consisted of a patio and some trees. My oldest started school, and we were close enough to walk. We spent a year and a half living in that condo until my parents bought a big-enough house which would allow us to move back in with them and have our own space. It was nice to be back in my hometown and with the comfort of my parents.

ABOUT THE AUTHOR

S tacie Carr is a thirty-five-year-old mother of three children: two boys and a girl. Stacie grew up in Ramona, California, and now resides in Landrum, South Carolina. She lives with her husband, Paul, and their three children. They have three dogs, ducks, and chickens.

CPSIA information can be obtained
at www.ICGtesting.com
Printed in the USA
BVHW081852200821
614852BV00007B/192